Go Beyond...!

Jimi Sheard

INSPIRATION TO PLAY

Beyond *the* Score

RELATIONSHIP KEYS
for GOLF *and* LIFE

JIM SHEARD, Ph.D.

IN HIS GRIP,
PLAYING THE GAME,
FINISHING THE COURSE,
A CHAMPION'S HEART,
THE MASTER'S GRIP,
FINGERPRINTS OF FAITH
and THE GOLFER'S BIBLE

Beyond the Score:
Relationship Keys for Golf and Life
by Jim Sheard, Ph.D.
ISBN 978-1-4507-3189-8

Unless otherwise noted, all Scripture quotations are taken from the Holman Christian
Standard Bible ®, Copyright © 1999, 2000, 2002, 2003 by Holman Bible Publishers.
Used by permission. Holman Christian Standard Bible®, Holman CSB ®, and HCSB ®
are federally registered trademarks of Holman Bible Publishers.
Note: The HCSB ® Golfer's Bible has devotional text quoted from The Master's Grip:
Lessons for Winning in Golf and Life, by Jim Sheard and Scott Lehman, J Countryman,
Nashville, TN, 2006, ISBN 1-4041-0385-6. This is a complete Old and New Testament
in a format specifically for golfers.

Cover and interior design by Lookout Design
Editing by Heidi Sheard
Many of the photos were taken by Doug Reuter.

jsheard@beyondthescore.net
www.beyondthescore.net

Beyond *the* Score

Beyond *the* Score

IV: DEMONSTRATE RESPECT
...to Show You Care

V: COMMUNICATE WITH PURPOSE
...to Strengthen Understanding

VI: SHARE EXPERIENCES
...to Achieve Mutual Goals

Introduction

Drive farther, chip closer, putt straighter; it all boils down to improving your score. Focusing on the score elevates performance, increases motivation, and encourages accomplishment.

But think about it. When you finish a round of golf, what is left? Undoubtedly, it is important to do your best and to strive to meet your potential. But focusing too intensely on results can keep you from a more fulfilling experience—the memories and relationships that last *Beyond the Score*.

> *We pay so much attention to the bottom line,*
> *the scoreboard, our score,*
> *that we miss out on the 'game' itself.*
> *In golf as in life,*
> *it's not so much the scoreboard,*
> *but enjoying the journey that really counts. Don't miss it.*
> —LEONARD FINKEL

The most important relationship of all is the one with God. He took the first step to initiate a connection with you by sending His Son. He will help you (1) connect, (2) provide value, (3) act with integrity, (4) demonstrate respect, (5) communicate with purpose, and (6) share experiences…with Him and others.

Develop and hone these relationship skills on the golf course, practice them in life, and experience the benefits. Play golf and live life *Beyond the Score.*

> *As difficult as they may be*
> *to establish and maintain,*
> *the friendships and relationships*
> *we establish and cultivate over the years*
> *are part of what makes life (and golf) enjoyable.*
> —GARY D. YORK & KEN OSNESS

> *God's definition of success is really one of significance—*
> *the significant difference our lives*
> *can make in the lives of others.*
>
> *This significance doesn't show up in*
> *win-loss records, long resumes,*
> *or the trophies gathering dust on our mantels.*
>
> *It's found in the hearts and lives of those we've come across*
> *who are in some way better because of the way we lived.*
> —TONY DUNGY, *Quiet Strength*

In achieving your goals, you must show strength by taking the initiative.

—JOHN ANDRISANI

INITIATE CONNECTION
...to Have an Opportunity

"LET'S PLAY GOLF!"

Connect with people with common interests to create opportunities for relationships to emerge.

Every relationship has a beginning. The key is to connect in such a way that you give the relationship an opportunity to grow and thrive.

Golf is a good place to initiate connection because a mutual interest in golf is common ground. Golf likewise affords opportunities to strengthen the connection and discover other common interests. The first three keys will help you create the opportunity for connection in relationships.

Take the Initiative

SOMEONE NEEDS TO TAKE THE FIRST STEP.

You must be alert, open, and alive to possibilities to make connections.

How well you connect is the first impression you make on another person. A warm smile, a friendly greeting, and an upbeat conversation will open doors to relationships.

Taking the initiative to meet another person is a risk that is often rewarded. But miss the chance, and you will never know what could have come from the relationship.

Ways to take the initiative in relationships:

Anticipate. Anticipate with *whom, when, how,* and *where* you will take the initiative.

Take a Risk. The downside of not taking the initiative is missed opportunity.

Take Responsibility. Your relationships are your responsibility.

Persevere. It is not enough to take the initiative. Be friendly, warm, caring, and selfless. People will respond.

ASK YOURSELF: When was the last time I took the first step to begin a relationship?

THINK ABOUT IT: Initiating connections is important for my success and happiness.

REMEMBER: I am responsible for my relationships, including initiating connections.

Let us not be content to wait and see what will happen, but give us the determination to make the right things happen.
—PETER MARSHALL

*There is a philosophy of boldness—
to take advantage of
every tiny opening
toward victory.*
—ARNOLD PALMER

*All human beings possess a desire
to connect with other people.*
—JOHN MAXWELL

*Keep asking, and it will be given you.
Keep searching, and you will find.
Keep knocking, and the door
will be opened to you.*
—MATTHEW 7:7

$\mathcal{F}$ind Common Interests

RELATIONSHIPS START WITH SOMETHING IN COMMON.

Mutual interests open the door for getting to know someone.

Common interests bring people together. Finding and cultivating a mutual interest is essential to a relationship. It is important to find the potential common ground and then do something to cultivate it.

Connecting Through Golf

There is great potential for connecting through golf. The pure challenge and joy draw people of varied back-grounds to the sport. Golf's initial attraction may be the challenge, but the opportunity for social interaction helps sustain people's love affair with the game.

ASK YOURSELF: How can I use a common interest to either connect with someone new or revitalize an existing relationship?

THINK ABOUT IT: Golf is just one of the common interests through which I can build a bridge to someone.

REMEMBER: Build on common ground to establish the bridge for lasting relationships.

*Golf is like fishing and hunting.
What counts is the companionship
and fellowship of friends,
not what you catch or shoot.*
—GEORGE ARCHER

*…fulfill my joy by thinking the same way, having the
same love, sharing the same feelings,
focusing on one goal.*
—PHILIPPIANS 2:2

Be Authentic

IT'S THE ONLY WAY TO BE.

Webster's Dictionary defines authenticity as "…conforming to fact or reality; trustworthy; not imaginary, false, or imitation." Authenticity helps build a solid base for what happens in a relationship. The goal should be to act and speak in ways that are genuine, veritable, and bona fide.

Distortion of Truth

We lack authenticity when we distort the truth about ourselves, intentional or not. Too often, in an attempt to paint the best possible picture, we try to impress or gain advantage. Some players claim their handicap is going up in order to complain or get sympathy. Or they may claim it to be better than it actually is in order to brag.

Authentic Relationships

Authenticity reveals our character and creates trust and connection with others. Leadership Consultant, Kevin

Cashman wrote, "The foundation of leadership is authenticity." Harvard Professor, Bill George believes authenticity is "being yourself; being the person you were created to be."

> *A round of golf allows you to get closer*
> *to fellow players than anywhere else.*
> *You and your partners soon learn—*
> *without a word being spoken—*
> *that what you're seeing*
> *is probably what you'll be getting.*
> —J. Brian Amster, Larry Salk,
> Craig Lockwood

> *Let your light so shine before men,*
> *so that they may see your good works*
> *and give glory to your Father in heaven.*
> —Matthew 5:16

ASK YOURSELF: What are my real motives in a potential new relationship?

THINK ABOUT IT: The more authentic you are, the more you respect yourself and those around you.

REMEMBER: A relationship without authenticity will fail.

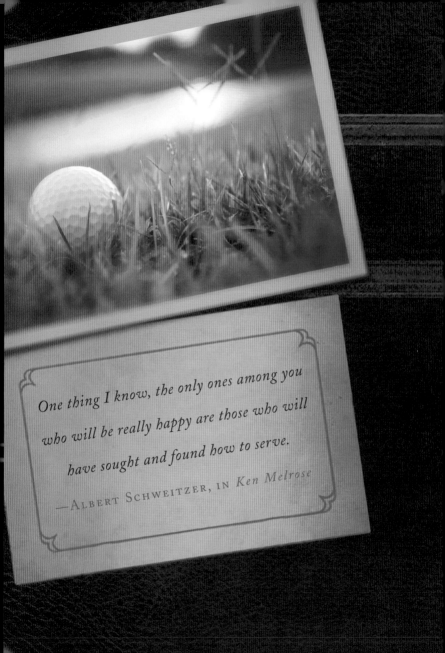

One thing I know, the only ones among you who will be really happy are those who will have sought and found how to serve.

—ALBERT SCHWEITZER, IN *Ken Melrose*

PROVIDE VALUE

...to Make a Difference

"BE MY GUEST!"

What people expect to get from a relationship must be perceived as a reasonable exchange for what they are willing to give.

An exchange of value must exist for relationships to survive and thrive. Think about your key relationships with family, friends, or business associates. For each person reflect on three questions:

What are you willing to give?

What do you expect to get?

Will it be mutually beneficial?

People appreciate being in relationships that meet or exceed their expectations. The next three keys show how to provide value to make a difference in your relationships.

ʃerve Others

SERVING IS GIVING VALUE.

Understand what the other person seeks, the value you can offer, then provide it and more.

When you have an attitude of service, the relationship can gain in significance and last a long time. Expectations are fulfilled.

A round of golf offers plenty of opportunities to serve your fellow players. Having an attitude of service helps you see the little things you can do, especially when a fellow golfer encounters a difficult situation such as a lost ball or a bunker shot.

Insights for serving others

1. You offer something unique: your time, your energy, and your talent.
2. What others value may cost you little time, effort, or money.
3. Give before you expect to receive.

4. Give more than you expect to get.
5. Service involves attitudes and habits for all relationships.
6. Invest yourself in people; you will be rewarded.

Customers First—Relationships Forever

If you're focused on "customers," the rest falls into place. That's why it's helpful to consider:

Who are my customers?
What do my customers expect of me?
How well am I doing? How can I do better?
Why do my customers buy from me?
Where should I focus to improve service?

> *How can I make people better*
> *as a result of connecting with me?*
> *...this is a strategy to connect*
> *with anyone, anywhere, any time.*
> —JEFFREY GITOMER

When will I make improvements?

With a little imagination, you can identify ways to provide more value and make a bigger difference in people's lives. The result will be deep, strong, long-lasting relationships with the people you care about most.

No other sport offers the potential of losing your ball while you are playing with it. Even more remarkable, golfers help look for an opponent's lost ball. This lesson of service points to the value of serving others in all walks of life to enhance business, social, and family relationships.

ASK YOURSELF: What can I do to cultivate a servant's heart?

THINK ABOUT IT: The simple act of paying attention can significantly enhance my relationships.

REMEMBER: What I give to matters more than what I get from my relationships.

The golf course, like the rest of life,
is a place where we need to be a blessing,
not a burden, to those around us.
—JIM SHEARD

Remember, in life,
you can never be too kind or too fair.
—BRIAN TRACY

Everyone should look out
not (only) for his own interests,
but also for the interests of others.
—PHILIPPIANS 2:4

Know Your Role

ROLES ARE EXPECTATIONS
FOR YOUR BEHAVIOR IN
CERTAIN SITUATIONS.

Knowing your role is critical to success in building relationships.

While there are the Rules of Golf and golf etiquette books which convey socially acceptable behaviors, expectations for behavior on the course are mainly handed down through experience in playing with others. Learning to serve others is one of the greatest gifts of the game.

Golf should be essentially a game of good fellowship; it should, and generally does, constitute a bond of union between strangers who casually meet.
—H.S.C. EVERARD, CIRCA 1890,
IN *The Golf Quotation Book*

Hospitality — Every Golfer's Role

An attitude of hospitality is a necessity for building relationships. There are opportunities to show hospitality every day at the golf course. Being hospitable can be rewarding because you enjoy the time, and others will enjoy being with you.

> *Don't neglect to show hospitality, for by...*
> *(showing hospitality) some have welcomed angels*
> *as guests without knowing it.*
> —HEBREWS 13:2

Role Expectations as Friends

Being a friend means connecting beyond the roles defined by your organization or group. Friends give and receive value from one another because they desire to do so, not because the organization expects it.

> *Friends help to complete us, and we'll be better for*
> *having taken them along on our journey*
> *to becoming all we are capable of becoming.*
> —JOHN WOODEN

Role Expectations for the Host

If you are hosting other people, the thoroughness of your plans and your behavior during the round will make the difference in your golfing relationships.

1. Understand your guest's interests and preferences.
2. Communicate plans to guests.
3. Clarify any payment responsibilities of guests.
4. Arrive early and welcome guests.
5. Focus on social responsibilities as host: greet people, make introductions, and avoid distractions.
6. Build relationships by planning teams thoughtfully.
7. Build in quality social time after the round.
8. Consider giving guests a memento.

Role Expectations as a Guest

As a guest you have opportunity to help build relationships with your host and other guests.

Express gratitude to your host.

Be gracious. Never complain or criticize.

Offer to pay for lunch, beverages, and tips.

Show interest in people. Be sociable.

ASK YOURSELF: How can I provide greater value to others at work, home, or on the golf course?

THINK ABOUT IT: Understanding my role in relationships should never be left to chance.

REMEMBER: An attitude of hospitality can go a long way in building meaningful relationships.

Do the Little Things

THEY ADD UP!

Your greatest impact may come from the little things you do for others.

Anyone who practices a few basic interpersonal skills will enhance their relationships. Making a difference in people's lives is not difficult or costly. In fact, it's often the little things that make the greatest impact.

(As a golfer) What is judged, and judged far beyond physical skill, is your presentation of yourself as an accomplished and secure individual. This means having a good knowledge of course rules, proper course-etiquette, when and where to engage other players in conversation, humor, patience, and playing a prompt, well-paced acceptable game.

—J. BRIAN AMSTER, LARRY SALK, CRAIG LOCKWOOD

Find Opportunities

The consistent use of your interpersonal skills helps other people feel important and appreciated. Those skills also help you gain value and respect in new and existing relationships.

Interpersonal Skills that Provide Value

Smile. It warms the space and people in it.

Remember and use names. People respond to their name.

Be inquiring. Ask about their favorite topics.

Listen well. Use all of your senses and your heart to listen.

Show genuine interest. Your sincerity will be obvious.

Be yourself. Do not try to be someone else.

Golf Etiquette Simplified

– Avoid stepping on a player's line.

– Fix divots, ball marks, and spike marks.

– Be ready to take your turn.

– Be still and quiet while others hit or putt.

– Congratulate a good shot.

– Keep advice to yourself.

– Rake the trap for yourself and others.

– Treat others with respect.

– Don't let your anger or excitement ruin someone's fun.

Acts of Kindness

There are small acts of kindness you can do for others on and off the course. One of the most common ways of showing kindness on the course is to help find a lost golf ball. But there are many others. All it takes is a desire to serve.

William Wordsworth considered the "little nameless, unremembered acts of kindness and of love" to be the best part of a person's life. Making others the center of attention shows you care.

Kindness for the Course

Watch shots. Follow the ball and note the spot.
Share your knowledge of rules. Be helpful.
Hunt for a lost golf ball.
Rake a bunker or replace a divot for others.
Pick up a club for someone.
Give encouragement and compliments.
Hold, remove, or replace the flagstick.

You have the opportunity to serve people in all walks of life— family, friends, business associates, and passing acquaintances. Through your acts of kindness, the little things you do for others, you have the potential to make a positive impact on someone's life.

The little things…

> **Add up…**
> **Mean a lot…**
> **Are always welcome.**

ASK YOURSELF: What is one thoughtful, unexpected thing I can do today to make a difference in someone else's life?

THINK ABOUT IT: If I give myself to others each day, I will never spend another day alone.

REMEMBER: Acts of kindness are small but have a big impact.

Respectable behavior on the golf course
is mostly a matter of common sense.
—MICHAEL CORCORAN

(Jesus said) 'It is more blessed
to give than to receive.'
—ACTS 20:35

He who pursues righteousness and faithful love
will find life, righteousness, and honor.
—PROVERBS 21:21

Golf is a game of integrity.

—RAYMOND FLOYD, In *Wally Armstrong*
WITH FRANK MARTIN

ACT WITH INTEGRITY
...to Instill Trust

"I'LL KEEP SCORE!"

Integrity is telling and acting upon the truth.

Relationships are based on two-way communication including written and spoken words, gestures, and actions. Integrity is based on consistent two-way communication. It goes beyond just telling the truth. It also involves "doing" the truth in a consitent manner. The truth about our ideas, beliefs, products, and organizations is at the core of a relationship built on trust.

Integrity, truth, and trust are important qualities for a golfer. Acting with integrity to instill trust is the theme of the next three keys.

Earn and Give Trust

EARN TRUST AND GIVE IT TO OTHERS.

Trust is a sign of faith and hope in the future of a relationship.

Trust is a two-way street. Give your trust to another person by using words and actions that reveal your acceptance of them. Gain their trust by demonstration of your integrity and loyalty. When you establish trust, you increase the potential to improve your relationship.

Trust is an important requirement in any relationship. It is also a foundation upon which other relationship qualities can germinate and grow-- freedom to fail, risk taking, honesty, and empowerment.

ASK YOURSELF: Am I trusted by others in my relationships?

THINK ABOUT IT: Take the lead by granting a degree of trust to others.

REMEMBER: Trust is based on accurate information.

Golf as a Game of Trust

Golf is based on trust. Until proven unworthy, a golfer is trusted to play within the rules. We trust others to count every shot and impose any penalties on themselves. We also trust the accuracy of their handicap.

Trustworthiness is a part of the fabric of who you are as a person. It is not an isolated action, but a part of your life. Since your behavior on the golf course tends to represent who we are in life, it is a good place to practice how to earn and give trust.

The only way of really finding out a man's true character is to play golf with him.
—P.G. WODEHOUSE, IN *Wally Armstrong*
WITH FRANK MARTIN

The role of a leader is really about relationships.
I spend 90% of my time on building relationships, build-
ing trust. And this [golf] creates the perfect venue for it.
—CEO of a Fortune 500 Corporation

Since you put away lying,
Speak the truth, each one to his neighbor.
—Ephesians 4:25a

Follow the Rules

RULES ARE PRESCRIBED
GUIDELINES, EXPECTATIONS,
OR BOUNDARIES FOR BEHAVIOR.

Following the rules is an indicator of a person's integrity.

We should strive to follow the rules. In golf and relationships there are consequences for our actions, including opportunity to build or lose trust. Our integrity is always on the line.

> *Golf is a rule-bound game,*
> *and playing means playing by the rules.*
> —J. BRIAN AMSTER, LARRY SALK,
> CRAIG LOCKWOOD

"Easy" Steps

Knowing and following rules enhances trust in relationships, sports, and life. To help you "follow the rules" in golf…

  a. Get a rule book. Carry it in your bag.
  b. Ask others how to properly handle situations.

c. Take time to discuss any rules questions.

d. Ask a golf professional to interpret the rule.

Actually, you can adjust the rules as long as your competitors agree in advance. Agree to play from the tees that suit your game, be flexible enough to enjoy yourself, and keep the game moving at a reasonable speed.

The game relies on the integrity of the individual to show consideration for other players and to abide by the Rules.
—USGA, THE RULES OF GOLF

Be careful to obey all these things I command you, ...because you will be doing what is good and right in the eyes of the LORD your God.
—DEUTERONOMY 12:2

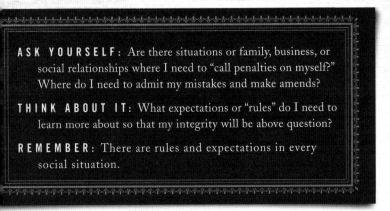

ASK YOURSELF: Are there situations or family, business, or social relationships where I need to "call penalties on myself?" Where do I need to admit my mistakes and make amends?

THINK ABOUT IT: What expectations or "rules" do I need to learn more about so that my integrity will be above question?

REMEMBER: There are rules and expectations in every social situation.

Exceed Expectations

GOING ABOVE AND BEYOND INSTILLS TRUST.

When you exceed expectations, you stand out from others.

Exceeding Expectations is going beyond guidelines or standards for performance. This includes stretching yourself to outstanding levels of service to help build strong relationships. Going the extra mile helps establish integrity and builds trust.

People who usually meet, and sometimes beat, expectations, can be counted on. They make good partners, friends, team members, and service providers. You can trust them and that helps strengthen the connection. You want to have relationships with those people. If you do the same, they will want to have a relationship with you.

Build Loyalty

Meeting expectations is fine. But exceeding expectations is the key to attracting and retaining customers in the highly competitive marketplace. When you go beyond other's expectations, they notice. Exceeding their expectation causes people to regard us in a more positive way. It is one way relationships can be strengthened through the game of golf.

ASK YOURSELF: What expectations can I exceed today, tomorrow, and beyond?

THINK ABOUT IT: Where would you score if your family members, friends, neighbors, customers, and colleagues were to fill out this service questionnaire on you today?

_____ Below Expectations

_____ About Average

_____ Exceeds Expectations

REMEMBER: Exceeding expectations includes little things, not just big, dramatic, one-time events.

All true golfers observe proper etiquette and the Rules of Golf voluntarily, with no one to police their actions except themselves. Players of all levels routinely call penalty strokes on themselves, the only game where it happens.

—MICHAEL CORCORAN

*If you paint in your mind a picture of bright
and happy expectations, you put yourself
into a condition conducive to your goals..*
—NORMAN VINCENT PEALE

*Rejoice in hope; be patient in affliction;
be persistent in prayer.*
—ROMANS 12:12

My father say (sic) to me,
'Respect everybody, and your life, it will be perfect.'
Then, even if you are poor on the outside,
on the inside you are rich.
—CONSTANTINO ROCCO,
IN *Golfers on Golf.*

DEMONSTRATE RESPECT
...to Show You Care

"I'LL HOLD THE PIN!"

Positive words and deeds demonstrate respect.

Respect is another two-way street. It is important to *show respect* for others, but also to *gain respect* from others. When you show respect for others, you demonstrate that you accept and value them through your words and deeds. To gain respect involves saying and doing things that show others you are worthy of their respect.

Respect is showing positive regard and believing each person has value. Without mutual respect, a relationship will not develop into something lasting and meaningful. The next three keys describe how to demonstrate respect and show you care.

Take Care of Yourself

TO GIVE VALUE TO OTHERS YOU
MUST FIRST VALUE YOURSELF.

Healthy self-talk is good for your game.

How you treat yourself has a profound effect on your attitudes, behavior, and success in golf, work, and relationships. A healthy respect for yourself helps you realize your potential.

I learned long ago that who I am
is not what I shot today.
—MARK BROOKS, IN *Tom Lehman*

People like to be with those who have a positive and realistic sense of self-worth. These people tend to be efficient, accomplish more, and bring out the best in those around them.

Self-Talk

Our relationship with ourselves is revealed through our inner dialogue. Too often we send ourselves negative messages about a shot we just made or the round we just played. Consider what you say to yourself before, during, or after a round of golf.

Since you are influenced by what you tell yourself, the messages can either set you up for defeat or prepare you to achieve your potential. Fortunately we are created with the capacity to value ourselves through self-awareness, positive feedback, and self-development.

We not only need to encourage others,
we need to encourage ourselves.
—JIM SHEARD AND WALLY ARMSTRONG,
Playing the Game

Build on Strengths

In golf and life, it is important to recognize, appreciate, and utilize your unique positive qualities. Build on your strengths. Make sure your limitations do not undermine your success.

Play Your Own Game

Each player ought to have a style
which is the reflection of himself,
his build, his mind, his age,
and his previous habits.
—SIR WALTER SIMPSON

Golfers are all different, and so are their swings.
—TOM LEHMAN

Play within yourself—play your own game.
—BILLY CASPER

Every golfer scores better
when he learns his true capabilities.
—TOMMY ARMOUR

ASK YOURSELF: How could I treat myself with more respect and admiration both on and off the golf course?

THINK ABOUT IT: What do I discover when I "count my blessings?"

REMEMBER: Play to your strengths on the course and in life.

You are what you think you are,
in golf and in life.
—RAYMOND FLOYD, IN *Tom Lehman*

Your chances of success in any undertaking
can always be measured by
your belief in yourself.
—ROBERT COLLIER

According to the grace given to us,
we have different gifts....
—ROMANS 12:6A

Care for Others

CARING IS SHARING SOME
OF YOUR VALUE WITH
SOMEONE YOU VALUE.

Treat others as you would like to be treated in the same situation.

Webster's definition of the verb *care* includes to be concerned about and to give care. Synonyms include pay attention, look after, keep an eye on, and keep watch. Our society admires those who care for others. Though you can't totally give yourself to everyone you meet, you can find ways to give care in relationships.

When you care for others you are:

1. **Attentive** – detect a real need
2. **Other-focused** – put others before yourself
3. **Creative** – add new ways to serve
4. **Satisfying** – receiver feels benefited

If you want to lift yourself up,
lift up someone else.
—BOOKER T. WASHINGTON, IN *Dungy*

It Really Shows

Caring fully about someone is demonstrated by genuine interest, putting yourself in their shoes, wanting good things for them, and acting in their best interest.

To show you care:

1. **Discover** what the person values, appreciates, or needs.
2. **Recognize** what you can give that will be valued.
3. **Determine** what you will do to meet his/her expectations.

You can show respect by asking others for their opinion, giving them your time and attention, dressing with respect for the person and situation, and offering to pay for something you share - like food, drinks, or golf.

Respect is one of the greatest gifts
you can give to another human being.
—ARMIDA RUSSELL

Byron (Nelson) gave me
his most enduring advice:
It's not how (well) you play,
it's how you conduct yourself
and how you treat people.
—TOM WATSON

Dale Carnegie once wrote that
the very best way to build
friendly relationships with others is
to become genuinely interested in them.
—BRIAN TRACEY

The second (commandment) is:
'Love your neighbor as yourself.'
—MARK 12:31

ASK YOURSELF: Do I care enough to give my very best to family, friends, coworkers, and golfing companions?

THINK ABOUT IT: What is it that I have to give that is valued in each of those relationships?

REMEMBER: Friends, family, and coworkers will care what you know when they know you care.

Embrace Differences

DIFFERENCES AMONG PEOPLE CREATE OPPORTUNITIES TO WIN.

Build upon your strengths and those of others.

To embrace differences is to actively welcome people who are different from you. Treating others with respect and dignity enhances your life. You may do it to benefit someone else, but do not miss the benefit to yourself.

Actively welcome golfers different from you.

- **Invite** a range of people to play.
- **Welcome** newcomers and guests.
- **Reach out** to those who may not feel embraced.
- **Utilize golf** to reach across age, status, or race.
- **Join groups** and leagues to meet others.
- **Play in events** where you will meet people.

– **Contribute** time, talent, influence and/or financial resources to organizations that promote diversity, such as The First Tee and Fellowship of Christian Athletes Golf Camps

Teamwork Works

Individual differences are evident in scramble (best shot) events. You quickly realize golfers vary in how well they drive, play long irons, chip, and putt. It is especially fun to be on a team with people who are very good at the parts of the game where you have weaknesses.

Utilizing differences helps create a team environment in which everyone can contribute, feel valued, maximize strengths, and minimize limitations.

For just as the body is one and has many parts,
and all the parts of that body, though many,
are one body, so also is Christ.
—1 CORINTHIANS 12:12

I have found the game to be, in all factualness,
a universal language wherever I traveled
at home or abroad.
—BEN HOGAN

You can do what I cannot do.
I can do what you cannot do.
Together we can do great things.
—MOTHER TERESA, IN *Maxwell*

Now there are different gifts.
There are different ministries,
but the same Lord.
And there are different activities,
but the same God is active
in everyone and everything.
—1 CORINTHIANS 12: 4-6

ASK YOURSELF: How can I embrace differences today?

THINK ABOUT IT: Have I been on a team where people with diverse skills achieved a challenging goal together?

REMEMBER: Embracing differences creates opportunities to make an impact.

The ability to communicate
is the most valuable of human skills,
and the one upon which
all relationships are founded.

—TONY LAKE

COMMUNICATE WITH PURPOSE
...to Strengthen Understanding

"GREAT SHOT, PARTNER!"

Communicating purposefully creates meaningful connections.

A connection is established at the beginning of a relationship. Building on that connection requires effort.

Primary to a strong connection is the quantity and quality of the communication. Skillful use of words, gestures, and symbols enable the exchange of economic and social value. The amount of value exchanged, level of trust established, and degree of acceptance granted to each other are key factors in strengthening understanding.

The next three keys describe how you can communicate with purpose to strengthen understanding on and off the golf course.

ᴀ̸sk Questions

QUESTIONS HELP YOU
CONVERSE WITH PURPOSE.

People love to tell you about themselves; just ask.

Conversations are the primary way we communicate in relationships. They include questions, answers, comments, body language, and gestures.

A round of golf is an excellent venue for conversation because it takes four hours to play, the setting is lush and beautiful, and there are gaps in the game that are conducive to conversation.

Converse with Purpose

By clarifying the purpose of the conversation in your own mind, and perhaps with the other person, you can be more focused. It will help you ask questions, listen, and encourage.

The purpose of any conversation usually falls in one or more of these categories:

Have fun. Pass the time. Enjoy each other.
Build connection. Get acquainted.
Provide encouragement. Support. Offer advice.
Exchange information. Share topics of interest.
Convince others. Persuade them to your point of view.

Questions with Purpose

Good questions show interest and encourage the other person to provide information. In *The Seven Powers of Questions: Secrets to Successful Communication in Life and at Work*, Dorothy Leeds describes seven ways questions are a powerful communication tool. They may be used to:

1. demand or encourage **answers**
2. stimulate **thinking**
3. give valuable **information**
4. put you in control and **help** people
5. get people to **open up**
6. inspire quality **listening**
7. get people **persuaded**

While they may be manipulative, questions can be used positively to show interest and gather information.

Questions are more likely to be seen as positive when they are:

Open-ended to encourage conversation.
Appropriate to the topic of conversation.
Thought provoking to invite contributions.
Well-timed for context of the conversation.
Positive and polite, to encourage response.
Balanced to give opportunity for contributions.

Examples of open-ended questions about golf:

How are you feeling about your game?
What's your favorite course?
How did you learn to putt so well?

ASK YOURSELF: What is my purpose in playing golf with this person today?

THINK ABOUT IT: What questions will improve the quality of our conversation and help us connect?

REMEMBER: When you converse with purpose you develop meaningful relationships.

Listen to other people,
keep interested in everyone else—
caddies and members and all.
Find out what they are doing
and what they care about.
—HARVEY PENICK

Healthy communication,
communication that fosters connection,
trust, intimacy, and respect,
is about knowing and being known.
—SUSAN CAMPBELL

Plans fail when there is no counsel,
but with many advisers they succeed.
—PROVERBS 15:22

Listen Up!

LISTENING SHOWS INTEREST.

Listen with open ears, eyes, mind, and heart.

Every conversation is an exchange of information, a give and take. Questions open the window to the person. Listening is the way we hear what is going on inside. In combination they build stronger connections with people. You develop opportunities to influence people and impact results.

Make a Difference

We all want to be appreciated and valued. We are attracted to those who listen because they seem polite, interested, and caring. They make us feel important and connected.

Listening is one of the best ways to show respect.

If you listen you will learn things that can help you achieve the important goals of your life and organization.

People have ideas that are valuable, but they need to be given an outlet to share them.

Listening is an important way to gather information about the person's opinions, interests, knowledge, and reactions to what you say. You have the opportunity to:

1. Strengthen **Relationships**
2. Generate **Trust** between People
3. Build **Commitment** to Ideas and Programs
4. Generate **Ideas** with Lasting Impact

Focus to LISTEN

Look Look at the person as you listen.

Inquire Inquire to show interest and clarify.

Seek Seek to understand. Be sincere.

Talk Ask questions, give feedback.

Encourage Encourage people to talk.

No Judging Have an open mind.

People want to know
*you **heard** what they said,*
*and **understood** how they felt.*

The greatest gift you can give another
is the purity of your attention.
—RICHARD MOSS, IN *Lehman*

O Divine Master, grant that I may not
so much seek to be consoled as to console;
to be understood, as to understand;
to be loved as to love.
—ST. FRANCIS OF ASSISI

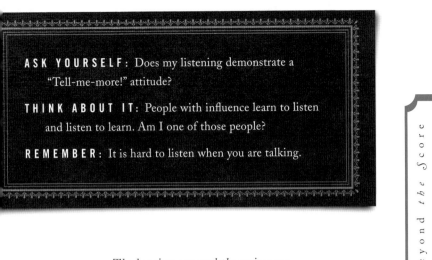

ASK YOURSELF: Does my listening demonstrate a "Tell-me-more!" attitude?

THINK ABOUT IT: People with influence learn to listen and listen to learn. Am I one of those people?

REMEMBER: It is hard to listen when you are talking.

The hearing ear and the seeing eye—
the LORD has made them both.

—PROVERBS 20:12

Encourage Others

BEING APPRECIATED IS A
UNIVERSAL DESIRE.

Sincere compliments cost nothing and earn great dividends.

Encouraging others on and off the golf course is something friends do for one another. It contributes to their well-being and benefits everyone. Tony Dungy, head coach of the Super Bowl Champion team, the Indianapolis Colts, wrote "God gives each one of us unique gifts, abilities, and passions. How well we use those qualities to have an impact on the world around us determines how 'successful' we really are."

How do we Encourage Others?

To encourage means to provide words, actions, or support which help a person believe in themselves and take positive action. The following are ways to provide encouragement.

Person's Need	How to Encourage
Feedback	Give Specific Examples and Observations
Encouragement	Offer Positive Feedback Replace Negatives
Support	Be Available to Listen, Discuss, and Help
Confidence	Give Lots of Praise
Decisions	Help Identify Options Review Pros/Cons
Information	Provide Information, Places, or Resources
Skills	Observe, Give Feedback, and Find Resources
Insights/Wisdom	Share Experiences Help Find Resources
Inspiration	Help See Possibilities Be a Sounding Board
Nurture	Express Care, Keep in Touch
Acceptance	Be Available, Provide Attention

Become an Encourager

Everyone has opportunities to encourage team members, coworkers, friends, or family members. The key is to identify **who** needs encouragement, **what** will be most helpful, and **how** to provide the support.

Too often we underestimate the power
of a touch, a smile, a kind word,
a listening ear, an honest compliment,
or the smallest act of caring…
—LEO BUSCAGLIA, AUTHOR AND LECTURER

Encourage someone today in your own style and in your own words and gestures. Try starting your next round of golf with this mental thought:

"What can I say, ask, or do
to encourage this person today?"

Encouraging requires being willing to:

Slow down. Step back and be available.
Notice. Be aware of others' needs and listen.
Focus on others. Develop compassion.
See priorities. See people above tasks.
Risk rejection. Get involved.
Have tools handy. Write notes of encouragement.

It's ironic, but golf encourages
this sort of atmosphere
where everybody pulls for each other.
—BEN CRENSHAW, IN *Golfer's Book of Wisdom*

ASK YOURSELF: Do I live by this motto? "Be liberal with praise." (espoused by Alan Loy McGinnis in *Friendship Factor*)

THINK ABOUT IT: You never help someone without benefiting yourself.

REMEMBER: Observe positive things about people. Encourage them.

*If you train your mind to search for the
positive things about other people,
you will be surprised at how many good things
you can observe in them and comment upon.*
—ALAN LOY MCGINNIS

*No rotten talk should come from your mouth,
but only what is good for the
building up of someone in need...*
—EPHESIANS 4:2

You may even remember to make out of each and

every round you play —

no matter what you score—

a mystical celebration of remembrance.

—M. Scott Peck

SHARE EXPERIENCES
...to Achieve Goals

"LET'S PLAY AGAIN"

Shared experiences nourish and sustain relationships.

By creating shared experiences that are enjoyable and valuable, you demonstrate your commitment to others. You also influence their commitment to you. Shared experiences that bond people may be once-in-a-lifetime events, but usually they are the accumulation of small moments of life experienced together.

Shared experiences are opportunities to interact with one another in a common task or activity. You have the opportunity, through shared experiences, to solidify connections in family, business, or social relationships. The last three keys show how shared experiences can help achieve goals in golf and life.

Build on Interests

G O L F   B R I N G S   P E O P L E
T O G E T H E R .

Seek opportunities to enhance your most important relationships.

Shared experiences are the things you do to build upon the foundation of common interests. They create new, lasting memories, and provide opportunities to give and receive value. It takes effort and a thoughtful strategy.

A relationship-building opportunity is an experience that …

> **fits** with your goals for the relationship.
> **enhances** the relationship.
> **builds** connection and commitment.
> **provides** value to the other person.

Building connections is sharing experiences
that make the connection stronger,
more meaningful, longer lasting, and more resilient.

Start them Early

Time together is a shared value at all ages. Families should develop these opportunities early in life. Spending time together reflects the priority of valuing the person, including kids. For many of us who love golf, it just happens to be golfing that brings us together. At first it may involve miniature golf or a small set of clubs in the yard.

> *The golf trip with friends may be*
> *the granddaddy of all golf experiences.*
> —W.P. RYAN, EDITOR-IN-CHIEF, *Minnesota Golfer*

"Wow!" Experiences

The beauty of the game and the camaraderie of the experience allows for many opportunities for golfers. A golfer relays the importance of his annual golf getaway to northern Minnesota.

> …the common thread—the bond that brings all forty of us together every summer for three days in June—is golf and the game's ability to help people enjoy each other's company, relax, and have fun. Playing golf with good friends and enjoying that time together is what brings us back to the same place every year and what makes it the golf highlight of the summer for all of us.

In the same issue of Minnesota Golfer, Jerry Clark, President of the Minnesota Golf Association, wrote:

> It is not about how you play, it is about the life experiences and acquaintances that would disappear if you were not a golfer… For me it would be overwhelming to even attempt to measure the loss of acquaintances, business practices and relationships, life lessons, friends, people skills, personal revelations and on and on and on.

When things go just right, it may be in an instant—a great shot, the sunset, or a beautiful photo—the word "Wow!" hits your mind. Sometimes these moments are orchestrated, and sometimes they just happen, but if you're lucky, you'll be a part of many "Wow!" moments!

ASK YOURSELF: "How would my life be different had I never been a golfer?" (Jerry Clark)

THINK ABOUT IT: Have I had a "Wow!" moment in golf or in life?

REMEMBER: "It is not about how you play, it is about the life experiences and acquaintances that would disappear if you were not a golfer." (Jerry Clark)

Whether it's a weekly game at your favorite course,
the after-work league with colleagues,
a charity event or an evening out with your family,
golf brings people together.
—JERRY CLARK

So rule number one
for deepening your friendships is:
Assign top priority to your relationships.
—ALAN LOY MCGINNIS

Don't neglect to do good and to share,
for God is pleased with such sacrifices.
—HEBREWS 13:16

Enjoy the Process

THINK POSITIVE; BRIGHTEN YOUR DAY AND YOUR GOLF EXPERIENCE.

Learn from the past; plan for the future; live in the moment.

We can learn from the past, make plans for the future, and enjoy the process. Life is meant to be enjoyed and that requires focusing on enjoying the here and now.

> *God says, 'I will take you…*
> *not where you want to go,*
> *but where you need to go.'*
> —ZACH JOHNSON, 2007 MASTERS CHAMPION

Friends and relatives make fun of golfers because they are so negative about the game they claim to like. We complain to one another and then use golf magazines, Golf Channel, friends, or golf books to find a quick and easy solution to the problems that plague our game. We are better off building on a foundation of positive thoughts and fundamentals.

> *Learn the fundamentals of the game*
> *and stick to them.*
> *Band-Aid remedies never last.*
> —JACK NICKLAUS, IN *Lehman*

Positive Golf Questions

Inquire into the Big Picture
What is the best part of my golf game?
What am I doing properly in my swing?
What are my strengths in irons, putting, etc?
How can I continue to develop my strengths?

Review My Round
What did I do best in my round today?
What positive things can I take from my round?
What did I enjoy most about the people?

React to a Shot
What did I learn from the shot I just hit?
How is that an improvement over the past?

Review Course Strategy
What were my wisest course strategy choices?

Positive "Swing Thoughts"

Overcome the negative by
focusing on the positive.
—JIM SHEARD, *The Golfers Bible*

I want an unhurried calm
in my golf swing…and in my life.
—JIM SHEARD AND SCOTT LEHMAN,
The Golfers Bible

…my goal every time I go play, is to have fun.
—STEVE JONES, IN *Steve Riach*

Do your best, one shot at a time,
and then move on.
—NANCY LOPEZ

ASK YOURSELF: When do I tend to get negative about golf?

THINK ABOUT IT: Are there parts of my life or work where
I would benefit from a more positive approach?

REMEMBER: Being positive about golf and life is good for
your results, enjoyment, and impact on fellow players.

I can sum it up like this:
Thank God for the game of golf.
Arnold Palmer,
—IN GOLFER'S BOOK OF WISDOM

You reveal the path of life to me;
in Your presence is abundant joy;
in your right hand are eternal pleasures.
—PSALMS 16: 11

Celebrate Golf and Life!

CELEBRATE, CELEBRATE, CELEBRATE!

Celebration is the commemoration of a relationship experience.

Consciously celebrating, even little accomplishments and occasions, can be a day brightener. It may be as simple as a coffee break together, a spoken "thank you," or a small gift. Celebrations, however small, add joy, memories, and meaning by calling attention to something good.

The best celebrations are about small gains, new relationships, and the good shots on the course. Even sharing a favorite golf memory with those who participated with you is like celebrating all over again.

Rituals of Celebration

People who take advantage of the opportunities to celebrate life have more fun, and are more fun to be around. Most people would benefit from more celebration in their life. Here are some thoughts about celebrating…

What to Celebrate in Life…

Accomplishments and achievements
Time and special occasions with friends/family
Life itself;
Momentary successes…congratulations
Teams and being a part of something bigger

What to Celebrate in Golf….

Victories and good performances
Improving handicap
Personal best
Great shots
Wise course management
Playing with special people and special places
Small contests like closest to the pin

How to Create More Celebration…

Have a positive attitude.
See joy along the way.
Seek different things to celebrate.
Be creative.

Celebration is about people, memories, and togetherness. It is also about keeping your eyes on the target.

Sometimes the goal is a winning score in golf, business, or other endeavor. At other times it is nice to help family members or friends feel special. There are many ways to say "You Are Special!" Let people know God made them unique, special to both Him and you.

Celebrate your own life. Enjoy yourself, utilize your talent, and encourage people.

Go Beyond the Score!

ASK YOURSELF: When was the last time I celebrated my accomplishments?

THINK ABOUT IT: Someone in my life deserves a congratulatory call or note.

REMEMBER: A celebration is the punctuation mark following a "shared experience."

A relationship with God is a process.
—STEWART CINK, 2009 BRITISH OPEN
CHAMPION

Business is Great!
People are Wonderful!
Life is Terrific!
—ROCHESTER FORD freeway billboard
in ROCHESTER, MN

These are the golden years,
therefore the golden days,
therefore the golden moments.
—HENRY DAVID THOREAU

May He give you what your heart desires
and fulfill your whole purpose.
—PSALMS 20:4

Follow-Through

Follow-through in relationships is like follow-through in your golf swing; it properly finishes what you started.

Basically, follow-through is doing what you said you would do. It helps prevent, identify, and mend problems that would otherwise damage a relationship.

Types of Follow-Through

Do what you say. Deliver on your promise.

Do your best. Follow-up to check on it.

Stay connected despite time and distance.

Be there when needed.

Check back to avoid surprises.

Adapt to needs.

Correct what is wrong.

Forgive and be willing to move forward.

Be humble. It can help heal a wound and mend a relationship.

*We are not so good
that we can get to heaven on our own.
We are not so bad
that we can't get there with Jesus.*
—Larry Moody, Search Ministry,
PGA Tour Bible Study Leader

Recovery Needed

As a golfer your hope is to hit a great shot every time. But inevitably, you will make some bad shots. Some will end up in the rough, the sand,, the water, or out of bounds. Bad things happen to every golfer.

When you hit a bad shot, it is obviously too late to do anything about that shot. But it is never too late for a great recovery.

After a bad shot, the most important one
is your recovery shot.

Recovery in relationships may not be quite that simple, but the principle is the same. Even when we do our best, we make mistakes. Once the mistake has been made, the most important action will be the next one you make. Try for a great recovery.

Three difficult, but necessary, phrases
help bring about the fresh start we all desire.
I Was Wrong…Forgive Me…I Need Your Help
—GARY D. YORK & KEN OSNESS

In golf, as in life,
it's the follow-through
that makes the difference.
—ANONYMOUS, IN *Jay Hall*

Epilogue

Lasting impact comes when you allow the Creator to use your gifts and talents to influence people. You can have an eternal impact that goes *Beyond the Score* as you Initiate Connection, Provide Value, Act with Integrity, Demonstrate Respect, Communicate with Purpose, and Share Experiences.

I hope people don't remember me for my golf.
I hope they remember me for my life.
—KENNY PERRY

I am able to do all things
through Him who strengthens me.
—PHILIPPIANS 4:13

Acknowledgements

Thanks to Renée Garpestad for her partnership in developing the initial format and content of this book. Her wisdom and enthusiasm for golf and life were a welcome influence. I learned a lot about relationships as I sought to understand these keys. Much of the credit goes to those who gave me the benefit of feedback. They include Heidi Sheard, my daughter-in-law and editor. My golf buddies Richard O'Meara and David Droog (deceased) taught me many life lessons. Like my family, they have helped me in my journey of relationship lessons. We all need a few of these patient people in our lives as we work to develop these relationship keys and move *Beyond the Score*.

Selected References

Amster, J. Brian, Larry Salk, and Craig Lockwood, *The Other Game of Golf: Practical Principles & Strategies for Business on the Course*, toExcel Press, iUniverse.com, Inc., Lincoln, NE, 1999, ISBN 1-58348-350-0, p. 5, 15, 17, 45.

Andrisani, John, *Everything I Learned About People, I Learned from a Round of Golf*, Alpha Books - Pearson Tech Group, Indianapolis, IN, ISBN 0-02-8643429, Dedication Page, p. xiii, p. 4.

Hall, Jay, *The Executive Trap: How to Play Your Personal Best on the Golf Course & On the Job*, Simon & Schuster, New York, 1992, ISBN 0-671-74575-1, p. 249.

Armstrong, Wally with Frank Martin, *The Heart of a Golfer: Timeless Lessons and Truths about Faith, Life and Golf*, Zondervan, Grand Rapids, MI, 2002, ISBN 0-310-24653-9 p. 175.

Campbell, Susan, *Saying What's Real: 7 Keys to Authentic Communication and Relationship Success*, An H J Kramer Book, New World Library, Tiburon, CA, 2005, ISBN 1-932073-12-4, p. xxi, 85.

Cantrell, Wes and James R. Lucas, *High Performance Ethics: 10 Timeless Principles for Next-Generation Leadership*, Tyndale House Publishing, Inc., Carol Stream, Illinois, 2007, ISBN 13:978-1-4143-0340 (hc), p. 127.

Cashman Kevin, *Leadership from the Inside Out: Becoming a Leader for Life*, Executive Excellence Publishing, Provo, UT, 2001, ISBN 1-890009-31-8.

Cink, Stewart, Search Ministries and Fellowship of Christian Athletes Banquet, PGA Championship at Hazeltine, August 2009.

Clark, Jerry, "Golf Transports Us," Minnesota Golfer, August/September 2006, p. 36.

Corcoran, Michael, *The PGA Complete Book of Golf: Lessons and Advice from the Best Players in the Game*, Henry Holt and Company, New York, 1999, ISBN 0-8050-5768-4, p. 321, 322.

Dungy, Tony, with Nathan Whitaker, *Quiet Strength: The Principles, Practices, & Priorities of a Winning Life*, Tyndale House Publishers, Inc., Carol Stream, Illinois, 2007, ISBN 13:978-1-4143-1906-3 (FCA edition.).

Flanders, Michael (Editor), *Golf Talk: The Greatest Things Ever Said About the Game of Golf*, Click Books, North Hollywood, CA, 1995, ISBN 0-9644693-0-8.

George, Bill, *Authentic Leadership: Rediscovering the Secrets to Creating Lasting Value*, Jossey-Bass, San Francisco, CA, 2003, ISBN 0-7879-6913-3.

Gitomer, Jeffrey, *Jeffrey Gitomer's Little Black Book of Connections: 6.5 ASSETS for Networking Your Way to RICH Relationships*, Bard Press, Austin, TX, 2006, ISBN 1-885167-66-0.

Golfer's Book of Wisdom (No Author), Walnut Grove Press, Nashville, TN, 2005, ISBN 1-58334-268-0.

Golfweek , September 16, 2006, p. 55.

Hobbs, Michael, Editor, *The Golf Quotation Book*, Barnes & Noble Books, New York, 1993, ISBN 1-56619-172-6.

Johnson, Zach, Search Ministries and Fellowship of Christian Athletes Banquet, PGA Championship at Hazeltine, August 2009.

Leeds, Dorothy, *The Seven Powers of Questions: Secrets to Successful Communication in Life and at Work*, The Berkley Publishing Group, New York, New York, 2000, ISBN 0-399-52614-5.

Lehman, Tom with Lance Wubbels, *A Passion for the Game, Bronze Bow Publishing*, Minneapolis, MN, 2005, ISBN 1-932458-35-2.

Lopez, Nancy, *Nancy Lopez's The Complete Golfer*, Contemporary Books, Chicago, 1987, ISBN 0-80924711-9, p. 209-210, 212.

MacRury, Downs (Editor), *Golfers on Golf*, General Publishing Group, Santa Monica, CA, 1997, ISBN 1-57544-023-7.

Nilsonn, Pia, Lynn Marriott, with Ron Sirak, *Every Shot Must Have Purpose*, Penguin Group, New York, New York, 2005.

Marriott Lynn, Pia Nilsonn, with Ron Sirak, *The Game Before the Game: The Perfect 30-Minute Practice*, Gotham Books, New York, New York, ISBN 978-1-592-40329-5.

Maxwell, John, *Winning with People*, Thomas Nelson, Inc., Nashville, TN, 2004, ISBN 0-7852-7636-X.

McGinnis, Alan Loy, *The Friendship Factor*, Augsburg House Publishing, Minneapolis, MN, 1979, ISBN 0-8066-1710-1, p. 22, 97.

Melrose, Ken, *Making the Grass Greener on Your Side: A CEO's Journey to Leading by Serving*, Berret-Koehler Publishers, Inc. San Francisco, CA, 1995, ISBN 1-881052-21-4, p. 157.

Moody, Larry, Founder of Search Ministries and Chaplain to the PGA Tour, Search Ministries and Fellowship of Christian Athletes Banquet, PGA Championship at Hazeltine, August 2009.

Penick, Harvey with Bud Shrake, *And If You Golf, You're My Friend: Further Reflections of a Grown Caddie*, Simon & Schuster, New York, 1993, ISBN0-671-87188-9, p.81.

Perry, Kenny, Search Ministries and Fellowship of Christian Athletes Banquet, PGA Championship at Hazeltine, August 2009.

Riach, Steve, *It's How you Play the Game*, Honor Books, 2001, ISBN 1-56292-893-7.

Ryan, W.P., Minnesota Golfer, August/September 2006, www.mngolf.org;, editor@mngolf.org

Sheard, Jim and Wally Armstrong, *Playing the Game: Inspiration for Life and Golf*, JCountryman, Nashville, TN, 1998, ISBN 0-8499-5433-9.

Sheard, Jim and Wally Armstrong, *In His Grip: Foundations for Life and Golf*, JCountryman, Nashville, TN, 1996, ISBN 08499-5329-4.

Sheard, Jim and Scott Lehman, *The Golfer's Bible: Holman Christian Standard Bible*, B&H Publishing Group, Nashville, TN, 2007, ISBN 978-1-58640-323-2, p. 564a and p. 1116w .

Sheard, Jim and Lenore Else, *Fingerprints of Faith: Evidence of Things not Seen*, 2009, fingerprintsoffaith.org.

Shemano, Gary with Art Spander, *Keeping on Course: Golf Tips on Avoiding the Sandtraps of Today's Business World*, McGraw-Hill, New York, 1997, p. 73, ISBN 0-07001628-3

Tracey, Brian, *Create Your Own Future*, John Wiley & Sons, Inc., Hoboken, NJ, 2002, p. 232, ISBN 0-471-25107-0.

USGA, *The Rules of Golf*, p. 1.

Webster's New World Dictionary of the American Language –College Edition, The World Publishing Company, Cleveland and New York, 1962.

Wooden, John and Jay Carty, *Coach Wooden's Pyramid of Success: Building Blocks for a Better Life*, Regal Books, Ventura, CA, 2005, ISBN 0-8307-3679-4, p. 43.

York, Gary D. and Ken Osness, *Master Strokes: Spiritual Growth through the Game of Golf*, Tyndale House Publishers, Inc., Wheaton, IL, 2000, ISBN 0-8423-3592-7, p. 30, 36, 48.